Seoul
Bus
Poems

Also by Jim Goar

The Louisiana Purchase (Rose Metal Press, 2011)
Whole Milk (Effing Press, 2006)

Seoul
Bus
Poems

Jim Goar

REALITY STREET

Published by
REALITY STREET
63 All Saints Street, Hastings, East Sussex TN34 3BN
www.realitystreet.co.uk

First edition, 2010
Copyright © Jim Goar, 2010
Front and back cover bus photos:
Robin (Wook-jin) Jang (Seoul, 2009) www.robinsays.com
Back cover author photo: Sang-yeon Lee (Norwich, 2008)
Typesetting & book design by Ken Edwards

Printed and bound in Great Britain by
CPI Antony Rowe, Chippenham and Eastbourne

A catalogue record for this book is available from the British Library

ISBN: 978-1-874400-46-2

Thank you to the editors of the following journals where some of these
poems first appeared:
*Can We Have Our Ball Back?, Cimarron Review, Copper Nickel, Ellipsis, el pobre
Mouse, Forklift Ohio, H_NGM_N, Harvard Review, Horse Less Press, Knock,
LIT, New Delta Review, Octopus, One Less, Poetry Salzburg Review, Snow
Monkey, The Bedside Guide to No Tell Motel, The Tiny, Typo, Watching The
Wheels: A Blackbird, & Word for / Word*
A special thanks to Jim & Elaine Goar, Tim Goar, Pirooz Kalayeh,
Loren Goodman, Marcus Slease, Stacy Dacheux, Matt Langley and Ken
Edwards.
Jim Goar

for Sang-yeon

I don't want to write
about leaves. The change in
seasons. my love. Instead:

The bell at 4:44 and by five.
silent. again. You've heard
it. Rain. Nothing poetic about
"she slept"

without a mother. a father. a mother. two brothers

4:01.
The monk begins to sing
"Good morning"

Not all bumpkins live in China

A lonely deacon
is hardly necessary for us
to cuddle full and belching
stars from afar
roll over and sleep with no
home I burrow constantly
meaningless I hope
the moon for lack of bananas
cramps that exhibitionist
can't be explained away

Witch doctors do not flinch
they run the city conjuring doves
and the doves are present and
on spindly legs
in the groin we call lice
holy in flight chasing down
the diminutive red and megaphones full of
chants on strike and workers left
to be mucked up pilgrims or
baffled Mohicans dancing around
and around
the lip makes good crystal sing

requiring this world
of short sight
to

sit
down

the Olympics are

out the window
and I'm

watching yr neck
in languages   and

have only
two eyes

for
taxonomy

emits
reception

a finely tuned retention

a Christmas carol boom

There must be something
on this mountain
top spinning
dizzy mewing
thirsty as hell
in sight of the ridge we
crawl in ports
of entry catch only
what others give can't
be shellfish with ornaments obscure
all motives in the rain
like chameleon skin blossom

Crocodile blood drawn
tight coils under pillows the
exhale will not
come ashamed or
still innocent she
says white I don't argue
socks need not scurvy
with a pack of wildebeests
running tatanka hands
my ears are soft horns and my owner
at two o'clock is not my owner at three
blocks of western migration
lemon rubbed teeth of cicadas
without venom she whispers
reptiles behind the knee

So what if bald turkeys stole your wedding dress
My darling
You look nice in that hospital gown.
And remembering your mother's scrambled eggs
But not her face
Isn't so strange;
Her eggs were good
And you have your father's eyes.
Just do me a favor, my suicidal rose
And get off the ledge
You'll kill the dirt if you fall.

I'm tired of
    the zoo

looking for my darling   dear
        when I cry,
        "Koo koo ka koo."

    you don't

        If acorns were sweet
        squirrels would be candy
     and squirrels are not
   in the trees
   from the west
          constellation that I love

        lay me a parrot down
        inside your warmest door

The washing machine
and no water the poem
without a bird without
Hae-yeon my darling the OJ is
warm and my coffee is no help

I live next to a
monastery bell that rings
33 times before sunrise
and 28 times at five

"the tutor's prince-nez lies upon yr
daughter's white breast"

I have forgotten so many lines this winter

The skin remembers how she crossed
and went away unpacked and stayed
where old times hang and spin
above a summer plane to thrust and fall
to dusk in early night she formed a couch
no longer heard
the oars of season shake and then
and out the sun at five o'clock
threw blind and shadows on my door
a strand of hair and reason break
the bindings of my nevermore

Ensconced
in the
bus   coughs
and I turn to
a barber shop   widow

smoke inside   snow tomorrow

scalding

cane and crane
reminders to shave

everywhere I look

This same corset
these same signs

inhaler and your breath
and your breath is yours

the seat is mine

20 million people live in this corner of my heart

I'm black   I've turned my
head   a torso manikin
who's dropped my stare

manikin manikin

wined and dined

in sooth   my mouth
     in blood   hot wood

If you didn't know
better
you'd say
something dead
lives in there
when you know
nothing of the sort
ever does
in the rain
what it feigns
in the sun

My wallet is on
    the floor
  carefully
  bend town

    before   sun
             became
             crass
 a plane
  shadow
 a bus
  shallow

  a passenger

       leaves

the curb   the street

    if a crosswalk provides
    if your eye   sprouts roots
  and those roots sprout atoms in ether

       be still

    means stay   while other wrists

 twist
 & mop

the light and love

  an illustrated bird
 more than the kind that crows.

Fair women

not painted   manger   find

to hide

this story explains

men ride buses
while men   ride buses

men

never move   the widow
the same seat   and pen

shirts cost more   one day   then the next

Opera of Korea
fish in the store   window

red lights
and around   more
red lights

This man of mud and marrow
decides to question the street
for no one walks
anymore they stroll with cranes
and hats removed an orange
poncho in empty flowers
that golden wake across the lawn
breaking little rakes akimbo
tree and mermaid song
a map under glass remembering

🚌

There is a list of names
outside my window.

In Changsha my name.
By noon the wall was
white again.

Nouns hang
from globes outside

my window. a list
of names outside
my window.

my name. the wall was
white again.

Nouns hang
from globes outside
my window.

the wall. a name
was white again.

The urge to speak about. rain.
just because. it is.
right now. as we. It
is. raining. raining. I could
tell you. the Coltrane.
the coffee. who knows? there is.
what did. that sound.

Constipation is an
occupation of wilting
umbrellas are never there
when you need them weeping
in the trestle a camera hidden is a
still daisy of remembrance that
black card played when lights
sleep we rest this journey
lies with paper instead of toes

sheets all filled with lemon
snow and everything is children
from the plant we tend music
of statues drip home open window
sleds of glass bird whose name
we do not know melt back and
forth in the tub a ducky quackady
quack on the bed you need another
shower of snow blue flower parted
this music is closest to German

Drummer. monk. my first coffee.
why all the noise? we are anxious
together. barking dog.

My room is behind the curtains. Good morning.
drapes are closed. Potholders. If I looked outside
I'd know. A funeral.

Five thousand Buddhas live next door.
I have not visited. them. they are
statues. milk cartons in the window.
wind and the absence of tin drums.

It is always today,
full of clarinets and coffins.
To a man
we answer telephones
afraid. We answer doorbells
instead of hiding. We accept "bonjour"
for "hello"
when they are not the same
at all.

The table has set
behind the hill and
at our feet full bellied
rest has eroded
speaking is done
on records a crow
asks so we are sure
to be breathing the last
of something inward a
cap screwed tight
an alarm in remission

Neither happy
nor fat bones
are waiting the dark
minced dry as the wish
broken tables and flowers
remember the one who
is not more food for ghosts
will starve without the living to serve

🚌

What's skin
today may not be

tomorrow's huskers
are growing today's

bits of no
always say
no

globes hang until
they don't

I am sure of the dust

my phone should ring.
anytime. you call

Meet you at time frozen
behind this door closed
to those who live
an empty circus a prowling
chameleon somehow warm
fades as do all words smaller
than a penny ring for the dead

While he plucked blues
she inserted a church
bell into his fiddle
to say that his tongue would not
be accurate or wine or just
playing with a room
around the loins and nothing else
was more like a brown
recluse in the pews one stocking
curfew I must get home
curfew I must I must
get home to curfew the bell
has sounded curfew my love
has sounded twelve times

Turn the egg over
it's still an egg
burn the egg over
and no one gets hurt.

spatula and the trash
played Sunday night

Men do not come till morning.

A pigeon broke its neck
against the cock of Ralph
the embalmer lapsed
displayed flowers
ate feathers and then the dish was
smashed up was swept up was
by taxidermy mounted from
trash reborn into a city
with cars on freeways and glue
to date eligible birds
or chicks if you must dance
heel to toe
in the background of a silent
picture eloping in early spring

a twist
a turn

here

a goose
there a goose
and goose
feel
not the dead kind
not the fish hung
nor
syllables
the whitest light
a fist holds
yet still
my hair falls

complaints

I'd like to apologize
(and do)
for dirty Hanes
bananas left up
hostess cards
grown old   a turn

pumping break
a turn
to the right
green bride
by my side

candlestick in the study

turn out the lights

no need to put

good money
after bad

🚌

There is no connection
between tomatoes and poets
and in light of this may I
rest a moment while tradition
shuffles like vegetables to raise
yr leg the stream continues
under bridges while bridges land
on this garden with only one eye

The blood will come and go
as children will go
out of the hamlet by a flute
played once upon a time
for style is straight or slightly bent
souls follow crumbs to the hut
where the oven is with tasty children
wrung dry of echoes the town falls silent
hails never weaken corn
shrugged and lost its yellow its
green a fire consumed
our houses of redemption

Words and now the silence
remains in blue slacks pressed
lemon and belly laughs
between a lover and his daughter
is her mother his lover
for crows to pick
a sieve from water dice
roll little boy yr brother
lost but no one calls to empty
crumbs along the way

The sand has moored
us we watch we
drift mostly we drift
in this sand watching
through eyes waiting to find
room outside waiting circling
still circling and everyone still

Today deserves pause
between still when read
a turtle beginning the girl outside
this slow drawl
just walking not strolling birds eating
interest is better kept curious words
stopped around goodbye

🚌

A ground the bend she climbs
buxom and apples in baskets
the collected breath of longing
when bouquets no longer will do
anymore is fateful as dice
in waiting you are the numbers
in heat you are the voice of citrus
she picks four moons to bake
a Japanese lantern on the table
predicates a ground hog in the den

The scope
a circumference

so full of grace

a green light and I've
no start at all

a biodegradable fist
and silk for shade

come sup with me

a   dusty floor

where no one stands
where

laundry drys

the bones inside
a thrush   a kite

ears bend the shelf

and inside shoes and
outside hands

a can of corn
a can of corn
a can of corn

Her vanity not her modesty
in question is always what
is your name and number two
came up and this was
the second take so
she let me get away with
my advances
filled with little people
you can imagine
the mess so I won't
bother a weeping soldier or
accost the demarcation line

How did knees
    touching dark   these joints
come running

                step

    ain't got no
that   ain't

                    mechanics of the   head
                            swivel
                                    round
                            some words   sans gin
            imply

        toes
    better than   any
        at the end
of a song
    who'll shine   my shoes

            white spit

    good pie

You were telling me about
the cliff behind the fence
you've seen the echo but
not the fall into the ocean
one foot at a time and the pants
will never come unless
you relax your monkey will
remain a coconut and sunshine
is all a man needs
in a tender heterosexual way off
where only the hounds go baying
at night the horses are eaten
questions asked by those
who stumble over rocks and
broken legs spring forth from
my beard my woman lives for this
rescue but I am not nor
do I need another

Divine night
look at me running between
rooms on lights turning off
the darkness I pause to look at
snow empty of something
I have in hand cannot be
an oak my bruised love

open a door
good neighbor

you should be
asleep

all night
through silk walls

the worm

inside
half under

my alarm clock

while rain
white rain

tunnels

beneath
the floor

🚌

No secret.

   garden.

in the rain.
transparent.

    waiting for

  what passes for

      classical music

       these days

The hummingbird in preference
a twig behind the daisy
prosaic and the clock is falling
letters those fuzzy red flowers
of no particular echo
through dunes heard a moment too
late rising in the brook
a moment too long
then away over morning weirs
hardly brighter than sugar cubes floating
plastic red waters the lawn

I haven't stepped outside. today.
I have no idea. if the drummer is.
waiting. that. was my loving. hand.
sincerely. the dawn.

If you need a man
walking white on water
you must be an island
hung out to dry
to sleep with one and
the other picking
secrets from the trunk
of dancing fingers bent
in gates where elephant
want the man to free
bananas and the ceiling
to look just at the sky

There is more   space than blue

can hold.   a hedge of lemon

a bookmark in mold.

these

two things appear

to appear

by glutinous

and prancer

by

sexton   \   the language

wears   down

the   well

of   rugs

dissemble

my memory   is shoddy

and I

have lost

the   train

is bleating

ink

an eye

to eye

a   bride

☗

snow moving
form exposed
          pipes

                    when all around
               the trees in my hair
                 my lovely locks
            at the moon and not above
                  the leaves
                going down

                              through sex we gain food
                         farm animal in bed
                                        make me nervous
                    shouting, "on Prancer" etc

          smoke stack   laughing

eye swollen   shut   purpose
                         slaps me shoulder
            shinning through
                              pearly whites
          from wherever there is
                 farmer
          (whatever that is)
               how now brown cow

                    my name is Jim
                 and the jungle
                 is filled with frost

Someone else   can freeze
   sunlight

        perfect day

  twilight till
     dark
   sent home

   look at me
I've forgotten to shave

         until now

    money would buy

      you
    this head to call

    and what you call

   day
after day

  my beating heart

    a scent
  I've never smelled

⊞

Beware the disconnect
between need   and movement
      cars parked

                        in the road
                there must be   mention
                  of airplanes   in childhood

            fantastic!

      To survive
            an empty stomach
            tomorrow   I turn   31

   denouement escapes
         moves to close
      how can end

                                    survive this

                  fast weep
                        close the book
                  draw a gun

            hand in hand
         how bright your dress
         how straight my lies

         action   hardly matters

                              after gin   you want the

                                    next song   or shrug

                     me

            fast asleep

Poetry series

1993

Kelvin Corcoran: *Lyric Lyric,* £5.99

Susan Gevirtz: *Taken Place,* £6.50

Maggie O'Sullivan: *In the House of the Shaman,* £6.50

Denise Riley: *Mop Mop Georgette* (O/P)

1994

Allen Fisher: *Dispossession and Cure,* £6.50

1995

Fanny Howe: *O'Clock,* £6.50

Sarah Kirsch: *T* (O/P)

Peter Riley: *Distant Points* (O/P)

1996

Maggie O'Sullivan (ed.): *Out of Everywhere,* £12.50

1997

Nicole Brossard: *Typhon Dru,* £5.50

Cris Cheek/Sianed Jones: *Songs From Navigation,* £12.50

Lisa Robertson: *Debbie: an Epic,* £7.50*

Maurice Scully: *Steps,* £6.50

1998

Barbara Guest: *If So, Tell Me* (O/P)

2000

Tony Lopez: *Data Shadow,* £6.50

Denise Riley: *Selected Poems,* £9

2001

Anselm Hollo (ed. & tr.): *Five From Finland,* £7.50

Lisa Robertson: *The Weather,* £7.50*

2003

Ken Edwards: *eight + six,* £7.50

Robert Sheppard: *The Lores,* £7.50

Lawrence Upton: *Wire Sculptures,* £5

2004

David Miller: *Spiritual Letters (I-II),* £6.50

Redell Olsen: *Secure Portable Space,* £7.50

Peter Riley: *Excavations,* £9

2005

Allen Fisher: *Place,* £18

Tony Baker: *In Transit,* £7.50

2006

Jeff Hilson: *stretchers,* £7.50

Maurice Scully: *Sonata,* £8.50

2007

Sarah Riggs: *chain of minuscule decisions in the form of a feeling,* £7.50

Carol Watts: *Wrack,* £7.50

2008
Jeff Hilson (ed.): *The Reality Street Book of Sonnets*, £15
2009
Peter Jaeger: *Rapid Eye Movement*, £9.50
Wendy Mulford: *The Land Between*, £7.50
Allan K Horwitz/Ken Edwards (ed.): *Botsotso*, £12.50
2010
Bill Griffiths: *Collected Earlier Poems*, £18
Fanny Howe: *Emergence*, £7.50

* co-published with New Star Books, Vancouver, BC

4Packs series
1996
1: *Sleight of Foot* (Miles Champion, Helen Kidd, Harriet Tarlo, Scott Thurston), £5
1998
2: *Vital Movement* (Andy Brown, Jennifer Chalmers, Mike Higgins, Ira Lightman), £5
1999
3: *New Tonal Language* (Patricia Farrell, Shelby Matthews, Simon Perril, Keston Sutherland), £5
2002
4: *Renga+* (Guy Barker, Elizabeth James/Peter Manson, Christine Kennedy), £5

Narrative series
1998
Ken Edwards: *Futures* (£O/P)
2005
John Hall: *Apricot Pages*, £6.50
David Miller: *The Dorothy and Benno Stories*, £7.50
Douglas Oliver: *Whisper 'Louise'*, £15
2007
Ken Edwards: *Nostalgia for Unknown Cities*, £8.50
2008
Paul Griffiths: *let me tell you*, £9
2010
Richard Makin: *Dwelling*, £15

Go to www.realitystreet.co.uk, email info@realitystreet.co.uk or write to the address on the reverse of the title page for updates.

Reality Street depends for its continuing existence on the Reality Street Supporters scheme. For details of how to become a Reality Street Supporter, or to be put on the mailing list for news of forthcoming publications, write to the address on the reverse of the title page, or email **info@realitystreet.co.uk**

Visit our website at: **www.realitystreet.co.uk**

Reality Street Supporters who have sponsored this book: